12K WORDS OF REALISATION

ADYASHA MISHRA

Published by InkQuills Publishing House
www.inkquills.in

First Edition 2022

ISBN: 978-93-90567-54-6

ACKNOWLEDGEMENT

I owe an enormous debt of gratitude to the people who have always motivated me and pushed me to write- my family and my friends.

This book would not have been possible without the help and efforts of InkQuills Publishing House.

My words in this book are authentic and straight out of my heart. It is not only based on my imagination, but also based on the stories and experiences I have heard from the people around me.

I can recall the days when my grandmother would narrate stories to me when I was very little. I used to listen to her every night before going to the bed. I also remember the times when I used to write poems and essays in my diary and made my parents read out loud and ask for their feedback and guidance.

This book might not be the one with extreme use of ornamental words and tough vocabulary, but I can assure you that these 12K words are the words I want to convey to the audience and make them feel good about themselves.

I am really grateful for every person and every situation that has made this book possible and I whole- heartedly hope that I am able to reach every heart through my words.

ABOUT THE AUTHOR

Adyasha was born in the year 1999 in a city of Odisha, Rourkela. Her childhood days passed in many states of India; Odisha, West Bengal, Gujarat and Uttar Pradesh. Because of which she now is able to speak languages of these states. All thanks to her father's transferable job. She currently lives in the capital. Since childhood, she is very creative as a person. She has learnt singing, dancing, sketching, etc. Since a very young age, she has been expressive through her words.

She loves to write about spiritual, inspirational, positivity and self-love topics. In the year 2020, she was a part of an Anthology book and got published herself for the very first time. Since then, she has been pondering to write a whole book all by herself. This is her first ever solo book. She got motivation to write from her Instagram followers. She used to put her thoughts on her social media status and people appreciated the way she expressed herself and made people feel about themselves.

She finds writing extremely therapeutic. She says that even if there is no body to listen to you, your notepad will listen. Just write it down. There's always a notebook and a pen in her bag, no matter where she goes.

She has done her BBA from Symbiosis International University and is currently pursuing her post- graduation from New Delhi Institute of Management.

She believes that no matter how busy your schedule is, you always find a way to do things you really love. That's why she keeps one or two hours aside from her tight schedule to continue her passion for writing. Since the past four years, she creates content on Instagram and YouTube. It enhances her creative side even more.

She has always kept her professional goals and passion separate. And she wants to grow and flourish in both the fields.

CONTENT

MY TEARS, MY LESSONS

Eagerly waiting to see the world,
I pushed myself out of mum's womb.
Looking at me through her weeping eyes;
She moved her fingers on my head just like a comb.

Years passed. She taught me all the good things.
Taught me to love everyone and said all are good human-beings.

When I was able to walk alone in the path of life,
I recollected what mum had said and got ready to experience every chapter of my life.

Met people with a smile, gave love and respect to them.
Did not receive the same. Was the problem with me or with them?

Still, I smiled with my heart in pain;
Walked with them in the brightest sun and even in the heaviest rain.

I left no stone unturned to make everything fine,
I let everyone bloom and everyone shine.

But what was I doing with me?
I cried more and smiled less.
I made everyone's life heaven, and mine, a mess.

Fed up with the daily mental trauma.
Decided to question about this to Maa.

When I said that she did not teach me the right thing earlier,
She smiled softly and wiped out my tear.

"How can I say that this world is made up of hollow
promises and plastic words?
You still are a little girl and yet to explore the whole world.
I might not be there to make you stand every time you fall.
You have to pass through every roller-coaster and take lesson
from all."

Crying my heart out over my faults, I hugged her tight.
Assured myself to never bow down under any circumstances
ahead, I moved from the dark to the light.

Clearing my brain and soul from all the sour memories and
bitter feelings,
Walked alone with pride.
Went towards the mirror with a spark,
Looked up and smiled wide.

YOUR PRAYERS AND SCREAMS

I know it's tough.

You are scared to go through the pain,

But at last you will always gain.

The heart you have is so pure,

You will get what you deserve, for sure.

Don't sleep every night with a heavy heart.

This night is ending, but every morning is a new start.

Do not let your soul feel the shatter,

Your mental peace and well- being does matter.

You are capable enough to achieve anything,

Attract all good vibes and keep the blessings flowing.

Why are you so sceptical about yourself?

You are moving correctly and desiring everything for thyself.

Of course, people will laugh at you when you tumble,
And that should be your motivation and not your trouble.

Shallow people won't ever understand your journey,
You are the master of your own life and your own attorney.

Don't chase everything, as, when you grasp all, you lose all;
Some paths will make you run and others will make you crawl.

Days are passing and you are getting closer to your dreams,
The God listens all, your silent prayers and even your powerful screams.

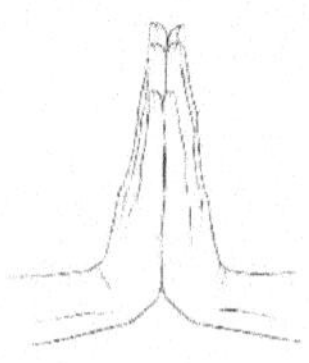

THAT SPECIAL ONE

There are so many people around you,

But your heart wants just one.

There are so many people in your contact list,

But you want a text only from one.

There are few people trying to get you,

But you are too focused on someone.

So many people can make you smile,

But nobody can make you feel like that one.

When your heart truly loves someone,

No one else is attractive to you anymore.

The room of your heart is occupied by them,

And then you shut the door.

That face soothes your soul like nothing else

Every other thought in your mind is somewhat scattered; but that love is extremely dense.

Now you know why people say that love makes you blind,

Because you blur the rest of the world and keep just one person in your mind.

And there's nothing wrong in doing that cause beautiful things should be held on;

Your warmth and consistency will surely make you two shine on.

I know sometimes things get complicated but miracles do take time,

Our heart knows the best, what's yours is yours, what's mine is mine.

The world is full of players, but you should be full of love,

Soon the morons will realize that people with tenderness and care are always above.

The seed of your love should be sowed with patience and solicitude,

Obstacles will come, you will weather the storm and have immense sense of gratitude.

GRATITUDE LIST

Grateful for the morning tea,

Grateful for the sunlight I see.

Grateful for the breakfast I eat,

Grateful for the people I meet.

Grateful for the music I listen to,

Grateful for the places I go to.

Grateful for the beautiful dresses I wear,

Grateful for the texture of my hair.

Grateful for the books I read,

Grateful for the days I bleed.

Grateful for the jewelry I got,

Grateful for the plants in my pot.

Grateful for the divine evening sunset,

Grateful for every fun I don't regret.

Grateful for the compliments I receive,

Grateful for the prayers I believe.

Grateful for the love I get from my dog,

Grateful for the things I write in my blog.

Grateful for the cool breeze of the nature,

Grateful for the pleasant smile from a stranger.

Grateful for everything I can afford,

Grateful for the places I have explored.

Grateful for the flaws I have,

Grateful for the strengths I have.

Grateful for the Almighty above,

Grateful for everything I do out of love.

Grateful for the fact that I am able to write this list,

Grateful for the fact that this life is a gift.

A NOTE TO EVERYONE

It's so good to move with the flow.

Absolutely anything in life…

Not to rush into anything, not to jump into a conclusion, not to overthink, not to burden your beautiful heart.

Life should be so simple and beautiful.

You are too young to be this stressed, darling.

I don't know why we want everything without having any patience.

Why do we torture ourselves to the point where we think giving up is the best option?

No, it isn't. You need to hold onto things that are important and make your heart happy!

Who said that you have to let go everything to be successful in life?

You can have fun, go to parties, make love, go to trips, doodle your favourite cartoon, make videos and post….

You can do all these without putting hindrance in your vision and execution to achieve goals.

All these sum up to what we call is LIFE.

These things are essential ingredients for the recipe of happy life!

You can't neglect happiness and love to reach to a certain level.

Learn to manage all these things. Life would be more meaningful and lovely place to live.

In this life, you can't always have everything.

There will always be some things that aren't falling in place perfectly. But that doesn't mean you will ignore the heavenly things you already have.

People often lose connections and love in this race because according to them, they can find love and peace anywhere.

Sadly, many don't know to hold on to the things that make them happy.

Never restrict yourself.

Let yourself feel everything around you.

Realise the good and the bad things happening in your

environment.

Don't just ignore.

In case something bad is going on, find the root cause and resolve it.

In case something great is happening, stick on to that and feel it.

There are all types of people around you

Only few deserve your importance or your company.

It is never too late to observe them and act upon it.

GIVERS ARE THE MOST BLISSFUL

If giving love, joy and happiness to people around you makes your heart happy, then do it without expecting anything in return.

Givers are always the happiest because seeing others happy makes their soul satisfied.

If buying little gifts, planning surprises, cooking something, pampering and expressing yourself in front of somebody makes you happy and excited, please do it.

But when you start doing things in a hope that you will receive the exact same in return, you will end up being disappointed in the future.

Therefore, it is so important to invest your time, efforts, money and feelings on someone who is actually worth it. Genuine and good people will put smile on your face even if they don't give any materialistic stuff. Love language of everyone is different.

So your expectations can't be fulfilled because you are expecting the way you give to people.

Every individual is different and their way of expressing and pampering is very different from yours.

And by saying this, I don't at all mean that you don't deserve those surprises, gifts and all the pampering, I just mean to say that it can't always be 50-50. Sometimes, it may be 70-30, and that is absolutely fine.

You are responsible for your happiness. People don't be with someone because of the other person's happiness, they stay because they themselves are happy. And two people come together because with each other, they are happier.

That is the real meaning of being with someone.

So let me again come back to the beginning lines, "Givers are always the happiest".

When you plan on something good and something special or even when you give your time, affection and efforts to someone, you are full of love and you want to give that to your person.

Believe me, not everyone is like this anymore. Not everyone is doing beautiful things without expecting something in return.

Even if the world is full of egocentric morons, you be the person full of love!

WHAT MATURITY ACTUALLY IS

I feel that the actual matured people are the ones who believe in humanity, good hearts, love and respect.

The ones who leave their past behind and forget and forgive no matter what all happened with them, those people are top tier. And not just forget and forgive, they meet people with the same love, warmth and gratitude.

Because they know that their current environment should not be punished for their past.

People usually tend to punish themselves by avoiding attachments, happiness, celebrations, love and positivity because they have the fear of loss which makes them believe that nothing in this world ever will stick by their side forever. It is not true.

There are things in your past. Those were lessons and those need to be forgotten. Those were needed but that's all, no other purpose was there.

SEE HOW BLESSED YOU ARE TODAY!

Welcome things and people with open arms, today.

Things do last forever.

You and I know it.

But that forever won't even start if you carry on the same burden from your past.

Some people are waiting to see you soon because they know how amazing you are. I think that's so beautiful. Give love another chance. Please?

If you take a chance today, maybe you will thank yourself in the next few days or months or years. Our lives are very different from one another. My journey is very different from yours. But what remains the same is that at the end, we all will get the love and care that we have ever desired for.

Just think for once.

If you can be so pure and so beautiful from within, then there must be someone like you who is made for you, who is just like you. The minute you realize that you are worth it and you will be blessed sooner or later, everything changes.

You will start seeing your life with a whole new perspective.

SOCIAL MEDIA'S DEFINITION OF BEAUTY

Today, we live in an era where social media is growing rapidly. Little girls and boys use Instagram or Snapchat for hours, daily.

Social media can be used to gain information, post pictures or videos, watch videos of their interests and what not. Just like every coin has its two sides, social media too has good and bad impacts on children/teens or the youths. The real meaning of beauty is changing day by day.

These little ones watch their favourite celebrities everyday and fall for their photoshopped or highly edited photos. There is nothing wrong to admire the pictures, but the problem arises when teens try to look like them. When they fail to replicate the models or celebrities of Instagram, they stress themselves by continuously thinking that they are not pretty enough or their bodies are not good or curvy/muscular.

It is so important to realise that there are so many people working on a celebrity's picture before it gets posted on their

Instagram handle. They are working so hard to make their picture look perfect or flawless. They are not just fixing the brightness or contrast of their pictures, they are even vanishing their acnes and blemishes, narrowing their waists, accentuating their curves, etc. Nowadays, anything and everything is possible with the help of editing.

Sometimes, social media makes you believe that you are not good looking enough if you don't look like a certain way.

It is also essential to know that a model's or an actor's job is to look charming because they all belong to Showbiz or glamour business. If they don't look good, nobody will cast them. So, to maintain their looks, they undergo trainings, do strict and extremely tough dieting, spend thousands or even lakhs on their looks.

We all don't belong to that business. We don't have to work in a movie. We don't have plethora of money to spend on our faces or our bodies. And to be honest, we don't even have to, unless and until you really want to be in that business.

It is great to invest in yourself, take care of the way you look. But it's not fair to yourself to replicate someone on social media. Everything you see online isn't real. People are working very hard to make it look real. But it's not.

Even I have decent number of followers on Instagram, I create videos, post pictures on every alternate day, post stories daily. In short, I am very active on social media. But I know that I don't have to look like someone else. I know that my body is perfect and my face is also fine. I know that I have some flaws and no matter how much I try, they will be with me forever because that's how I was born. So sometimes I am very conscious about my looks and other times I feel like there is nothing to hide or feel shy about.

Having said that, I also believe that commenting or taunting your friend or sibling on looks is not very pleasant to do. Even if you do it in a fun way, you don't know for how long your words can stick on someone's head. It may affect them badly and they will definitely start overthinking it.

If you really care about someone's looks, there's always a fair and pleasant way to let them know. And it is always better to not say anything negative about how a person is looking or what a person is wearing. It is always a good idea to appreciate them and show some kindness.

They might be draining their brains already by thinking about their bodies daily. No matter how much someone has awareness about body positivity, he or she definitely overthinks or at least aspires to be in a better shape.

Let's be kinder to our people around.

You can never go wrong while appreciating someone's looks, someone's body.

Let's change the definition of beauty the way it was earlier where people didn't stress about how they are looking every hour of the day…

WHAT A PERFECT DAY LOOKS LIKE

So, tell me what comes to your mind when you think about a "perfect day" in your life?

Is it about an extremely productive day at your office? Is it about a road trip with your family and friends? Or is it about just sleeping the whole day and eating your favourite snack?

I will tell you mine. My perfect day is all about some work, some rest and some quality time with my family and friends. And my definition of a "perfect day" will change daily. But a perfect day will always look "happy". The happiness you experience during the day will give you a satisfied feeling which will make you say- "What a day it was!"

So the key ingredient of a perfect day is you being happy in everything you do. If you want to make every day a perfect day, you need to find happiness and positivity everywhere possible.

But now you can ask me that- “How is it possible to stay happy every hour of the day? We are humans and we sometimes get upset or tired or sometimes we even cry!” Those days can also be perfect. I will tell you how. Let’s take an example.

Suppose your boss yelled at you in the meeting today in front of your colleagues and you are feeling abominably bad. All you can think about is that meeting and you are unable to focus on other things.

This example is very common. Isn’t? As individuals, we have different ways to feel things. So people be upset or act differently when they are in sorrow. Some stay silent, some cry out, some even take out their irritation and anger on family. It is obvious that the incident will make anybody bothered and dismayed.

I believe that we should definitely allow ourselves to feel things. But sour or bad memories should be let gone as soon as possible. So let us come back to how you can make such a day a "perfect" day. Half of your day is gone and the rest few hours are all yours for you to change everything. It is difficult, but not unachievable. Just think about what are the things or activities that totally cheer you up. You have to do it for yourself because you need to be happy for that "perfect" day. Always try to find the root cause behind any bad experience. It can be the other person, or sometimes the reason can be you too. After analyzing or knowing the cause keep that memory aside. Don't let that eat you completely and ruin your whole day. And then do things for your own happiness. If playing golf or cricket makes you the happiest, do it. If going out for a movie is what excites you usually, do it. If you think that sharing your problems with your wife or your mother can help you overcome your stress, then do it. Do anything and everything that will help you make your rest of the day, the best of your day. And it is very much possible unless and until you yourself want to do it. Some people don't even like to talk or do anything after such an incident. They come back to their home and sleep with a heavy heart. Of course, it is totally based on personal wishes and choices. But here, we are talking about how to make any day a "perfect" day so that you feel satisfied before going to the bed and feel a lot better. And a happy mind gives you better solutions to your problems.

According to research and science, "when you smile, your brain releases neuropeptides which are tiny molecules and they help you to fight stress."

Also, according to a study, the people who were very happy had an IQ between 120-129. And the people who were not happy had an IQ between 70 and 79. So now you can yourself see the difference.

"You feel better, you think better."

Therefore, first find happiness around you, smile more, cheer yourself up. Then, automatically you will resolve your problems all by yourself, because by then your brain's ability to grow and expand has already been done.

If I talk about myself, I usually try to play with my little sister or with the kids in my neighbourhood. We play ludo, carrom, cards, etc. Kids really cheer you up. They take all your worries away just like a magic. That's my way of beating stress. Your way can be completely different from mine. So, make sure to stay happy! Make sure to beat your worries and stress in your own way.

Remember: A PERFECT DAY LOOKS VERY HAPPY.

BE MODERN, BUT DON'T DUMP YOUR VALUES

As years are passing, we are getting more inclined towards the western culture.

If you ask me, I would say that some things should never change no matter how many decades pass. It's perfect to think or be in the original traditional way when it comes to few things. This thing totally depends on perspectives. Some won't agree to my point for obvious reasons. And that is totally understandable.

But, according to me our traditional or old thinking/mindsets give more importance to "value".

Value to relationships, value to culture, value to feelings, value to our origin, etc. I believe the meaning and significance of the word "value" is slowly fading away from our lives. And this is because we now have many options for almost everything. "Having a little inconvenience or bad phase in your marriage? Alright, get a divorce and marry someone else.

“Want to look modern and cooler? Stop believing in God and forget about your culture and origin.

“Your friend is not texting you first? You don’t initiate it either. Get some new friends, meet new people.

Why all these are happening?

Only because we now have many options and we want to feel “modern”.

Getting a divorce is okay. Breaking up with somebody is fine. But not giving the bond a try or refusing to adjust is not fine. It shouldn’t be okay. But the sad part is, it has become okay to not adjust. When two people come together, they are likely to have some difference of opinions because they are different individuals. But if you really want to be with them, some adjustments are needed. That’s how bonds work. Unless and until someone’s behaviour is intolerable or disrespectful or toxic, you should work on the connection and value them.

Secondly, on a regular basis I witness that people are now drifting away from their origin and culture. Their belief in God, their belief in festivals and their knowledge and awareness about their culture is slowly sinking. You can be "modern" while praying, while celebrating.

"Modernization" has nothing to do with dumping your values. To be called as a person with a broad mind has nothing to do with forgetting about your origin or beliefs. In a race to achieve so many things in today's world, I believe that we all are collectively responsible for this.

I am not saying to achieve less or not aim high. Being ambitious is wondrous. But a successful person with great values has a different level of aura altogether. I think it is very attractive.

So let's not forget our roots. We all are here for a purpose and the greatest purpose is sticking to our values. Working on relationships and friendships is much more important than going gaga over new people every day. How on Earth is it possible for you to find good genuine people every now and then? It is not possible.

I was watching a Bollywood movie few days back and I heard the actor saying that "ek chhoti si baat pe main usse chhod ke bhaag jaaun? Agar chhoti- chhoti baaton pe insaan ek dusre se bhaagne lage toh kya farak hai hum mein aur jaanwaron mein?"

And this can hit anyone. It means that if we run away from each other in small- small things, then what is the difference between we humans and the animals?

If you feel that you are somewhere not connected to your roots and values anymore, then give it a thought and try to find the connection again! It totally depends upon what you want and your personal choices, but if you felt good after reading this, then believe me, you are thinking very right. You believe that values are important and when you adapt or return to your values, everything changes for the better.

HUSTLE > EXCUSES

You will never be a hundred percent ready for anything. There will always be a reason to hold you back no matter what you are trying to do and no matter how headstrong you are. So, there will never be the "perfect time". You don't have to wait for too long for that time.

You won't ever be completely ready to invest in stocks.

You won't ever be completely ready to start a new business.

You won't ever be completely ready to commit to someone.

You won't ever be completely ready to start a healthy lifestyle.

There's no such thing as perfect time. You make the time perfect by your own decisions. You do justice to the time by choosing what's right for you. You do it for yourself when you realise that life is too short and uncertain, so the right time is NOW.

Let us take one situation from the things I have mentioned above.

"You won't ever be completely ready to start a healthy lifestyle".

You want to start it. You want to be fit. You want to look in a certain way. But you can't start this lifestyle if you keep on thinking:

"Junk food excites me so much; I can't switch to healthy stuffs".

"I will have to wake up early every morning but I have always been a lazy person".

"My schedule is very tight; I have a lot of assignments to do. There's no time for gym or exercise".

And the list goes on and on…

If you start thinking about the excuses you can make to yourself for not starting a healthy lifestyle, there will be many. So as a result, you tend to push your goals away. You procrastinate. You sabotage your own self-confidence and self-esteem by thinking that you won't be able to do it. On the other hand, people are actually doing it every day without making any excuse to themselves.

Don't they have cravings for junk food?

Don't they have assignments to complete?

Don't they feel lazy sometimes and wish to sleep a little more?

They go through these thoughts on a regular basis. But they don't let these become a hurdle or barrier in achieving what they really want. When you really want something, there are lot of risks or obstacles associated with it. And these things will always be there. And that is the actual challenge. That is your test. Whether you let those hurdles overpower or vanquish your goals or you stick on to what you actually want and work for it.

That's the whole point.

In life, we want so so many things but we end up pushing it away by our own excuses. And that's the reason we keep on changing our goals. We could not attain our previous goal, that's why we keep switching between our desires or dreams. Our goals fluctuate. And as a result, we never succeed.

Therefore one thing you need to ask yourself when you are planning to achieve anything: Am I going to accomplish it with full commitment and hustle or will I let my excuses overpower my goal?

FORGIVE YOURSELF

Why forgiving yourself is so important?

Holding yourself accountable and punishing yourself for a very long period of time is not good for your personal growth, no matter what mistake you had committed and how enormous that was. When you ruminate so much about an incident or that mistake of yours, you leave no room for positive thinking and self- improvement.

What you should do in this case is simply accept that you were wrong, apologize if you have hurt someone and most importantly- FORGIVE yourself. I sometimes overthink, curse and punish myself after committing mistakes. But then it is very important for me to realise that one mistake doesn't define me as a person.

It is essential to learn and grow from that mistake. If I repeatedly do that mistake, then I should ponder enough and get my actions or mindset correct. It is never too late to realise things and act upon it. But don't be late to forgive yourself. I have learnt this in my life. There were days where I used to grieve and cry so much over any mistake that it had become impossible for me to live those days happily, with a smile on my face. The more you think about your mistakes and punish yourself, the more you push yourself away from actually working on your growth. Having said that, by no sense I mean that one should totally forget about their faults or mistakes.

Nobody forgets. Nobody should cover their sins or mistakes and refuse to accept that they were wrong. Realise. Hold yourself accountable. Think about brighter or positive aspects. Work on your self-growth. Committing mistakes are normal. No matter how hard you try, sometimes you just can't avoid few things. It's impossible to be perfect. Therefore, do it for yourself. Forgive yourself with a smile and assure yourself to never repeat that thing again. This is so important for your mental peace.

When I write "mistakes", I don't mean anything too awful, cheap or atrocious, like murder, harassment or something that is not right in front of law.

Those are not mistakes, those are crimes. And these shouldn't be forgiven or forgotten. Of course, the criminals or evildoers too need to work on their mindsets and help themselves to become a better person, but there are few things you can never undo and you deserve a severe punishment. Anyhow, we are not talking about the "so- called mistakes" that a criminal does (which are actually crimes). These people are too shallow and the law will take care of it.

We are talking about the actual mistakes like: Shouting on someone because you were angry, accidently disrespecting someone, doubting somebody, using inappropriate words that could offend people (when you say without an intention to hurt the sentiments), etc.

There are plethora of other mistakes that we commit unknowingly on a daily basis and we deserve to make ourselves better by accepting our faults and working on ourselves. You will come across people who will remind you about your mistakes after you have started to work on yourself positively. It is true that nobody can change or forget what you had done or how you behaved earlier, but don't go to the flashback and start overthinking again. Now, you are much better than what you were earlier. You have come far. You already have thought a lot about it. You apologized very sincerely. You promised to yourself and to others that you won't ever make them feel down. The people who genuinely care about you and who know that you are working on yourself, they will forgive you. They will believe you. They will have faith in you.

And you don't have to think so much about what other people might be thinking about you. It is normal to feel embarrassed after any mistake, but when your heart knows that you are really sorry about something and you have apologized to people with your whole heart, then trust me, you don't have to think every time about what they are thinking about you.

Sooner or later, they will forgive you. You have to stand by your words and bring change in your actions. Not to prove anybody else, but to yourself. When the change begins inside you, you start witnessing changes outside you. It all begins with you.

TWO WHOLES, NOT TWO HALVES

You have definitely come across the statement- "He/she is my better half". People usually use this to describe their partners.

But I feel that we all should start saying- "He/she is my other whole." We all are born "complete" or as a "whole", not as halves. When you start believing that you are half of someone, then you also start feeling that you actually need the other person to complete you. You are complete. When two people come together, it is because there are lot of similarities, lot of good vibes, understanding, adjustments, love and care. And all these traits are present inside every individual. We just wait for the right person to show these things to.

So, by no means we are halves of other people. We are a total package with or without the "love partnership" or "companionship" of another person. It is too important to feel fulfilled and complete in your own-self before you try to build your life with somebody else. Some people actually find their missing parts in other people. It is true that finding a person who encourages you and takes care of you is more than a blessing, but feeling that you are nothing without them and you need them in every step of your life is not at all true.

Nothing is missing from you. Nothing is lacking in you. Nobody in this world can complete you. If you keep on believing and relying on other people for their contribution in your growth, then you won't be able to do anything on your own if the Almighty puts you in a position where you are alone. When you are too dependent on other people, you forget how capable you are.

So, if you are of the belief that you have a "better half"; it is very sweet of you to think that way. But I do think that saying that isn't fair for both the people. We all should replace it by "other whole", without lessening our love or respect for our partners. This won't bring any evident change or twist in your relationship, but it would boost your self-esteem as an individual. At the end of the day, we should be happy in ourselves. We should feel complete and fulfilled, irrespective of the fact that we are with or without someone.

People should change their mindsets otherwise they will keep on settling for less and they will keep doubting their own abilities. I am nobody to burden my opinion on you but according to my belief, one must always take his or her decision on their own. I recommend or suggest everyone to think, analyze and decide about situations on their own. Trust your gut and don't let anybody overpower your thinking. Don't let anybody manipulate your decisions only because you think that another person means so much to you.

Love is beautiful. It teaches you so many different things. But on the other hand, I also feel that enjoying your own company, being comfortable in your own skin and being your own number one priority are also very important things.

No matter how much someone loves you or cares about you, they can't be with you every minute of the day. But you are with you every day, every minute, every second.

"YOU ARE COMPLETE. YOU ARE WHOLE."

Start believing this from today itself. Because it's a fact!

HARRASMENT: EVERY GIRL'S STORY

Are you a woman or a girl who is scared to acknowledge the fact that you have been treated in an inappropriate manner by someone?

Because I am not.

I am not scared. I am not even one percent sceptical while writing that "yes, I have been mistreated and made uncomfortable at 2-3 points in my life." I don't recall it every now and then because (by god's grace), those incidents were not too awful or traumatizing for me. The situation could have gone worse if I didn't have presence of mind. Thankfully, I could use my brain at the right time and take necessary steps spontaneously. Now, why am I saying/writing all this?

Every morning you unfold the newspaper, you get to see at least 2-3 cases related to harassment or sexual assault, little girls being mistreated in schools, etc.

If you are a woman and you are reading this, ask to yourself where and how you were made to feel uncomfortable. I am sure you will be able to recall at least one incident. If you are a man, ask your sister, wife, mother, daughter, or your friend if she ever has gone through such incident in her life.

Some women will accept in front of you if they feel like. But most of them won't even open their mouths to accept that people have misbehaved with them. They want to keep it within themselves. They feel ashamed, scared and uncomfortable while sharing those feelings with you.

It is so unfortunate that the victims have to suffer for so long when incidents like these take place. But the culprits roam freely and joyfully because we refuse to take actions against them. Some become so silent after that page of their lives that even their parents remain unawarded about it for the whole life. When you share those things with someone, it will actually reduce your sadness and make you feel better. Because, it is so obvious that an obnoxious incident like that will cross your mind every hour of the day initially. You won't be able to focus on your day to-day work or activities. You don't deserve that. You don't have to burden your mind or soul with that thought. So let it out. When painful memories are shared with the people who love you, the sorrow actually becomes extremely less. You feel very light. Even if you don't want to take any action against that person, you should share it with your closer ones.

But I would suggest to take necessary actions against that person. At least you can try. Try for yourself. If you and I keep calm then the culprits will get more encouragement and target or hunt new people.

That's not what we want.

We want change. We want safety. We want a peaceful mind. We want other people to feel safe too. So, do you think your quietness will bring any change?

And it is so important for the parents to teach their children about what is right and what is wrong. I feel so bad while writing this that these little children should know about good and bad touches and listening to you about these harassments and incidents. But I think that it's the need of the hour. The best we can do is spread awareness as much as possible and take precautions and stay vigilant everywhere.

My parents were always very open to me about all these. Therefore, I never hesitate to open up to them. So, that comfort in relationship is very important. Make sure to maintain that kind of relationships. Make your near and dear ones very comfortable so that they feel free to communicate anything and everything with you.

Also, cases can happen with anybody, irrespective of their gender. Hence, it is not only important to educate little girls about these, but also boys should know everything about these.

Some parents feel very awkward to ask or talk about sexual harassment, abuse or good and bad touches with their children.

Especially the fathers. But your children go to schools, travel through metro, go to restaurants, visit their friends' houses, etc. And let me tell you, bad people are present everywhere. You and I don't even know about it. So, children or teens should be prepared well by their elders. As a parent, you might feel hesitant, but it will only bring positive changes and it will make your bond even stronger with your child if you speak to them about these topics.

I always share everything with my mother.

I don't feel ashamed or awkward while telling something to her because she has made me feel that I am her best friend. So, just like we share our secrets with our friends, I share my whole life with her.

We people live in Delhi and we usually travel by metro and we know that we do find different types of people in the metro train. Some of them are very cheap and they touch you inappropriately by taking advantage of the rush.

Once I experienced this too. The train was very congested and a man came and stood behind me. He actually didn't stand behind me, he got stuck to me. I got very angry but didn't react. I got scared too. I decided to step down in the next station. When I came outside the train, I realised that he too stepped out. He was starring me from a distance, in the platform. I rushed to my place, I told everything to my mother. To be honest, I was not scared in the metro because I knew there were hundreds of people present there and he could do nothing more or worse. But nobody has the right to even touch you without your consent. I should have scolded him or asked him to stay a little distant from me. I should've spoken.

But at that time, my presence of mind told me to step out in the next station, take an auto and reach home. This was the best I could think of.

Every place is risky. We should have balls to stand for ourselves. We should keep an eye on everybody. My mother always tells me, "you should always look at people with doubts.

Ask yourself that why someone is being so nice to you. Think and keep your eyes, ears and brains open, always".

All the people are not like you darling.

Their intentions are not always right. You need to save yourself every time.

Therefore, if unfortunately, you are going through any kind of thought like this or if someone is misbehaving with you in your workplace, school, college or even at your house, please speak up.

They are nobody to do this to you or make you feel that way.

I know every girl has experienced some kind of harassment. But it shouldn't be "normal". People shouldn't say that "ye sab toh hota rehta hai". Bad things should not be normalized at all. We need to bring an end to these things.

The things that should be common or normal are kindness, standing for your rights, speaking and sharing about topics like these, love and support.

If not now, then when?

EXISTENCE OF GOD - IS IT FOR REAL?

Are you a theist or an atheist?

Do you believe that someone up there is taking care of you and guiding you the right path or protecting you from mishaps or adversities?

Prior to the pandemic, in the year 2019, a study was conducted in India to find out what percentage of people believe in God. The results showed that nearly 97% of Indian people do believe in God. They believe in their existence. And this was a general study and included people across all the religions.

According to my research, there are roughly 4,000 different religions in this world. Yes, even I am stunned after knowing this. But that's true. We don't have idea about what religions actually do exist beyond the 5-6 religions we have heard about.

Nearly 75% of the world's population belongs to one of the 5 religions:

Christianity, Islam, Hinduism, Buddhism and Judaism.

But according to recent studies, Sikh community comprise around 0.38% of the world's population, that is higher than the percentage of Jews (0.23).

These are the religions that we are familiar about. We know people who belong to these groups.

Now, you must be wondering that why am I talking about religions. Because, I will be talking about beliefs and diversity. Starting from different holy books of these religions to the festivals they celebrate, everything relates to God.

Let's get to know about the sacred texts of the major religions:

- Hinduism: The Vedas and Upanishads
- Islam: The Quran and The Hadiths
- Christianity: The Bible
- Sikhism: The Guru Granth Sahib
- Judaism: The Tanakh and The Talmud
- Jainism: The Agamas

These sacred texts are also known as "scriptures".

These are the writings with regard to the worship of the deity.

Here, by no means I am trying to discriminate or compare the religions. All I am doing is to let you know that people like you and me, irrespective of our religion, believe in God and worship in our own ways. We might not have seen the God, but we do feel the God.

If I am in pain or fear, or when I feel too happy and grateful, I visit the temple to seek blessings. My Sikh friends visit the Gurudwara. In the same way, Christian people go to Churches and Muslim people visit the Mosques.

Little amount of our population doesn't believe in God and doesn't visit holy places. I know they think that it is better to stay away from all these because they believe that Gods don't exist and if something isn't visible to them, they don't trust it. That's totally fine. People have their own choices, beliefs and perspectives.

But let me tell you, there have been numerous studies on this. There have been proofs that the things mentioned in the scriptures or holy books, once actually existed. Well, there's no such concrete experiment you can do to detect God, but there is nothing wrong to believe in the Almighty. There's nothing wrong to feel that you are being guided well by someone up there and you are never alone.

I whole- heartedly believe that I am being blessed, watched, protected and guided by Bhagwan ji. I do believe that if you want or need something and you pray for it, the Almighty will bless you for sure. There's an energy above science.

When you and I are out of control or totally helpless, I feel that God shows us the right path by taking control over.

Even if someone is an atheist, God is with him/her. He is taking care of us. I have nothing to prove, but my belief is above everything. Just like everyone else's.

LOOKING EXPENSIVE HAS NOTHING TO DO WITH MONEY

Do you know that you can present yourself in such a way that you can make heads turn irrespective of the fact how much you have spent on your look or from where you have shopped from?

Do you know that you can look absolutely amazing without spending massive money?

Nowadays, everyone has great awareness about body positivity and embracing yourself just the way you are. But no matter how much you read positive quotes or train your mind to love every bit of you, it is impossible to be a hundred percent confident and secured in yourself every time.

My only suggestion to people would be that if you think that you have some flaws (which is normal, everyone has it), that makes you feel that you look less attractive, then try and be "presentable" every time. No matter what skin tone you have, no matter what your body shape is, no matter what your face features look like…Be Presentable every day!

Present yourself in such a way that you forget about your insecurities. Dressing up well, smelling good, taking care of your hair and nails, smiling (always), maintaining your posture while walking or sitting, etc are so important things that are actually underrated. If you want to look pretty or handsome-take care of yourself. And for that, you don't have to be a spendthrift.

You have to realise that there's no direct connection between money and you looking amazing. Of course, there is some relation, but even if you don't invest a lot of money in something, you will still feel amazing and expensive.

When it comes to your clothing or your wardrobe, the collection should be all about your personal choices and how you want to look. Most people buy stuffs because they want to invest in trending pieces, which is completely fine, but they don't know how to carry themselves in it.

I could be wearing a jacket from Versace and no one might be looking at me and on the other hand, I could be wearing a dress from the street market and I might be successful in making the heads turn. Therefore, it's all about how I carry myself, how well I present myself. Most of the time, it has nothing to do with how much of my hard- earned money I am spending on my overall look.

High- end products excite everybody. I too love to watch videos on YouTube that are related to luxury handbag collection, shopping in a luxury brand store, etc. And it makes me feel that one day even I want to build my own luxury collection wardrobe. It pushes me to realise that if I want all these, I need to put my shoulder to the wheel and earn a lot of money so that I would be able to have that kind of lifestyle.

But it is not necessary that only those products or collection will make me look rich or presentable. I try my best to mix and match the pieces from my wardrobe and create new looks.

I think that the colours you choose to buy are also very important. I have realised that neutral colours like beige, nude, off-white, white, black, etc make you look more classy and more expensive. These colours are aesthetically pleasing and never go out of fashion. When you are unsure about what colour to wear, go for these neutral colours. Trust me, you can never go wrong with these colours.

Also, I feel that it is about where you are visiting.

If I am going to a beach or a picnic, I can experiment with colours and opt for something fun. I can't do a neon orange or pink for a professional meeting. So, it is all about the place I am going to.

I don't know if it's a myth or something, but some people think that good quality products can only be found in luxury stores. If you have shopped from normal street markets, I am sure many times the quality has amazed you. I have seen great collection in these street markets.

Who am I to stop you from not choosing a high-end brand? Nobody. I am nobody. It's all about our choices. But all I am willing to convey through this is that you can look perfect and rich without investing a lot. You can find better alternatives and options to style yourself in these markets.

Coming to the self-care part, I feel that people notice your toe nails, hair, the way you smell, how clean and tidy you are, etc. If I want to style my hair for an event and want to make it look more healthy or shiny, it doesn't mean that I need to go to a huge salon and spend thousands. If I have time, I would rather do a DIY hair mask at home which would be inexpensive and natural too. It would give similar results. Using curd/eggs/ aloe vera on my hair can bring better results as compared to any salon. I even do my own manicure at home and do my own nail art and keep it presentable. So, I try to do everything that I am capable of doing myself. This not only saves my time and money, but also brings out the creative side of mine.

Also, to be very honest, I don't have crazy amount of money that I can spend on my looks.

But that doesn't hamper my personality. That should not be an excuse for me to not look presentable. It's my responsibility to carry myself well with everything I have right now. No one else will do it for me. Maybe when I become financially independent, my choices would change. I would be able to actually spend more, but even that time I would know how to look presentable and spick and span without spending much.

YOUR BRAIN IS YOUR FIRST HOME

Where do you spend the most amount of time?

In your house? In the office? No.

You spend most of your time in your head. Or I should say that you spend most of your life inside your head.

No matter where you are sitting, where you are going, what you are doing; you live most of your life inside your head. Hence it becomes extremely essential for you to make your mind a peaceful and amazing home to live in. And only you are capable of doing that.

No matter what your external environment is, your internal environment should not be disturbed. Because, you have to live inside you head for long, very long. You can't afford it to be an unpleasant place.

People should practice PMA (Positive mental attitude). It affects every kind of behaviour of an individual in a good way.

Thinking about the greater good no matter what the circumstance is, requires a lot of positive thinking and great mental attitude.

Usually, people carry and practice "neutral attitude". These people usually tend to ignore their issues and always depend on other people to come and solve those issues. They have a balanced approach.

But a person with PMA, doesn't depend on anyone. He or she has a habit of looking at every situation with lot of positivity and with a happy mind. They have the ability to self- evaluate every situation and focus on the brighter side.

That is the reason they have the potential to immediately jump back and overcome after hitting the rock bottom.

We all go through challenges and face tough situations every day. So, just think if you make your mind a peaceful and good place to be in, almost all your problems will get solved by itself because you would have greater capacity to think and analyse everything.

You are the most important living person for you. When you think better, you live better. I know it is impossible to think everything positively. But at least we can try. We can try till it becomes our habit. And once it becomes a habit…Boom! Life becomes smoother and easier.

Your mind will always think the way you want it to think. You have control over your mind. Don't let the mind control you. You know, there are voices in our heads. Some are positive and some are negative.

If you experience a lot of sorrow, pain, jealousy, doubts, anger, frustration, stress and anxiety on a regular basis, then you have a habit of listening to the negative voices in your head. The positive and negative voices in your head are your own voices. People speak to themselves every now and then. So, if your days are not making you feel happy and satisfied with yourself, then you are most probably in a bad habit of practicing negative mental attitude.

I will say this again, "You live most of your life inside your head." Your mind should be like a garden. Full of greenery and colourful flowers. And if by any chance, the leaves and flowers of your garden become dry, water them. Make them alive again. It is never too late. Do everything to maintain the life of your garden as long as you are alive.

It is better to start practicing positive mental attitude as early as possible. If children or teens start thinking and focusing on brighter aspect of every situation, then their lives will become much better and much easier in the long run. Therefore, the earlier you start practicing it, the better your life becomes.

When you start thinking that everything in your life happens for you and not to you, life gets a lot more meaningful. Everything changes and you start evolving as an individual.

MEANING AND SIGNIFICANCE OF "KARMA"

The whole world today knows the word "Karma". This word is derived from the Sanskrit word "karman" which means "act".

The meaning of this word is: The result of an individual's actions, as well as the actions itself.

It is basically the cycle and process of cause and effect.

According to people, they first witnessed this word in the Rigveda (the oldest Hindu text). And today, every little child knows about this word. This small word has such a deep meaning associated with it. I feel that it is a complete sentence in itself. People today know that their actions, the way they treat people, their behaviour and deeds, all have an effect and everything comes back and the cycle goes on and on.

If you do good to people, you will receive happiness in unexpected ways. If you do bad to people, you can't escape from the fact that one day, sooner or later, you will get hurt too. Everything returns to its original giver. If your intentions towards someone are not pure and you exploit them, then eventually you will be made to feel the same way by someone else or that person itself. It is all planned. It's all written. But no one else writes it for you. Your own deeds decide your destiny.

There's a story in Ramayana. Most of you have already heard about it.

The story of Shravan Kumar and Dashrath:

Shravan Kumar was a man who was very unfortunate that both his parents were blind. He would carry them on his shoulders in balance/scales like structure or device. They desired to go on a pilgrimage.

When they reached the forest, they felt very thirsty and asked their son to get some water for them. On that day, the king of Ayodhya, Dashrath, was out for hunting in the same forest.

Dashrath was great at hunting. He had the ability to aim from miles away. Shravan reached a river named "Sarayu" to collect some water for his parents.

Dashrath heard the sound of water when Shravan dipped the vessel in the river. Dashrath mistook it as the sound of a deer drinking water. He aimed and shot the arrow and it pierced into the chest of Shravan. The King rushed to that place after hearing the painful voice of the boy. He informed the King that he had come there to get water for his parents. Shravan asked Dashrath to inform his parents about his death.

Dashrath took some water for them and informed them about Shravan's death. They were devastated.

The King took them to the place where their son had died. They cursed King Dashrath for killing their son. They took dip in the sacred river and died in the same place. They had said that one day Dashrath would also face the same.

The curse was found to be true because the King couldn't bear the pain that his son, Lord Rama went on exile for fourteen long years. He waited for Rama for some while but couldn't wait more and then took his last breath. He too suffered the exact pain that the blind parents of Shravan Kumar went through.

You see here that, though the incident was completely unintentional, the King of Ayodhya got his Karma. He got punishment for his deeds. He didn't want to kill the boy; he had gone there to hunt animals. Even killing innocent animals for fun and to show the world how powerful you are, is a sin. But on that day, he made a greater sin by accidently killing

Shravan Kumar. Even though it was an accident, the damage was done. And when any damage is done, the consequences are to be suffered, sooner or later.

I had to mention about this story because it is a great example of Karma/Karman.

What did you learn from this story?

Ask yourself and find out the answer. It is all about your personal learning.

It is important to care and not hurt the feelings and sentiments of other people. Once you do it, you can't take it back. All you can do is realise and try to become a better person. What is done is done. And what's done will come back in unexpected ways. You never know when and where you will get your karma.

Therefore, if you want a happy life, you need to keep others happy. It's as simple as that. You do good, you get good. You do bad, you get worse.

If you have always done good to people, loved them unconditionally, prayed for them, treated them well, never exploited them, never hurt them, then just wait. Your blessings are on the way. Some people need to have patience because they deserve much bigger and much better blessing. It will come to them.

I have heard a lot of my near and dear ones say that, "I have always been good to people, but they always leave me and go. They don't treat me according to my expectations. Why does it keep on happening with me?"

I have two answers for that.

First, you need to wait. Maybe you deserve a love deeper than the ocean or simply, they don't deserve you. Therefore, God is planning something greater for you. He will keep on removing people from your life until he blesses you with someone that genuinely deserves the kind of love and care you bring to the table.

And second, you are getting your Karma.

You know, there are few actions that we have done unknowingly. We didn't realise because we were unable to see our own actions or hear our own words. Maybe we had hurt someone from our past but we had no idea because they didn't react. We all have done mistakes unintentionally. We all have done some sin and have zero idea about it. So maybe that could be the reason that you are unhappy now. You think that you are perfect and you do everything without hurting the sentiments or feelings of people, but that's not true. Maybe in the present you are a much better version of yourself. But you might be getting your punishment from the past, today.

As I said it is a cycle. And we have to suffer in this birth itself, in this life itself. There's no escape. So next time you see yourself breaking down and crying, do yourself a favour by ruminating and realising what had gone wrong in the past. Realise and then wait for your blessings and happy moments.

If you are unable to recall any such action of yours that was hurtful or bad towards people, then just have patience.

God is preparing you for greater things in life. He is going to bless you in the most unexpected way!

POWER OF MANIFESTATION AND LAW OF ATTRACTION

Do you believe that if you keep on thinking about something and give out energy to the Universe, then you can actually attract that thing or that wish towards you?

You can literally attract anything and everything towards you with the help of manifestation. I don't know whether it is based on the spiritual belief of a person or someone from above knows what you need and gives it to you. But it is true that there is a lot of power in manifestation and law of attraction.

It is not a short process. You can't get anything all of a sudden or immediately. Your consistency and working towards to get that thing is very important. You are not just supposed to think about what you want. You also have to work towards what you want. That is how manifestation or law of attraction actually works.

It is basically the personal belief of people and the attraction they create. Manifestation is much more than positive thinking and willpower. If you have something in your mind for yourself and you want it in reality, you need to manifest it. You need to be very clear about what you want or desire. To own your wish, you first need to know your wish, clearly. People desire different things in life. You might want your soulmate and I might want a great job. Our desires are totally different.

Once you know what exactly you need, you need to inform the Universe. The Universe has to know exactly what you need because the Universe itself will provide you the thing you will be manifesting.

You can inform it through different ways. You can speak out loud, but from your heart.

"Yes! I got this. I will get this job. I will work here." Or even better is, "I got this job. I am working in my dream company. I deserve this."

You can use any of the two sentences according to me. In the first statement, you are talking about your future. You are positive, but you are saying that you will get that job. On the other hand, the second statement is much more confident. You already said to the Universe that you are working in your dream company and you deserve every bit of it. I don't think that this is over-confidence or arrogance. Because, you are extremely determined and you have every right to motivate yourself.

If you want to work in a certain company, visualize yourself working there every day. This brings us to the second way of manifesting, visualization. When you visualize yourself with your goal or your dream, your confidence gets even more stronger. The people who are looking for their soulmates, they visualize their partners to be in a certain way. Their looks, behaviour and other characteristics. We all are visual creatures. We create picture in our heads. This is a good way of manifesting. We create blueprint or we have a rough idea about what we are looking for.

You can also pray. Praying is such a therapeutic way of asking the Universe to give what you want. You believe that someone will bless you if you pray. Praying and meditating will bring peace to your body and soul. It gives you the opportunity to dive deeper in your own thoughts. When you are calm, you think much better. The people who practice meditation regularly, have a better idea and better picture of what they want.

Now, once you know what your goal is, you have to start working towards it. The Universe or God will help those, who help themselves. You just can't ask for it. You need to earn it. Nothing is for free, or no one is too lucky to get everything they want without working for it. Efforts matter everywhere. Efforts, consistency, hard work, positive thinking and so many other things bring you closer to your dreams. It is a regular process.

I might visualize myself of becoming the CEO of Google, but if I keep on lying in my bed the whole day and do nothing to be in that position, do you think that I will become the CEO ever? I really need to pull up my socks and get grinding. I can't leave everything to the Universe. The Universe won't feel like helping me if I don't stay focused and determined.

Your role model or idols have surely manifested once in their lives. They wished and prayed for it, they worked for it and they are grateful for it. Remember to always thank the Universe after you get what you had manifested for. The happiness you are getting is because of the combined hard work of you and the Universe.

You can never go wrong by thanking and being grateful for everything.

So don't wait for too long. Manifest it today. Manifest anything and work towards it with your full dedication. You keep your focus on yourself and your goals and watch the Universe help you at every step of your journey.

LET THE DUST SETTLE

We all experience uncertainties and difficult situations every day. We are never prepared for those. Life gives us shock every now and then. The most important part is, how well do we handle those situations.

People have fights with their near and dear ones, people lose their money all of a sudden, people go through bitter experiences. Initially, everything feels worse. You don't know what to do or what not to do. Your anger, anxiety or regret heightens in this phase. Mostly, the overall thought process of people itself gets bitter. And that results in every other situation or behaviour of that person. Knowingly or unknowingly, he or she damages the other aspects of life, at least for a while.

But when a person believes that sooner or later, the dust will settle down and everything will return to it's normal position, then it becomes easier for that person to handle every kind of uncertainty or situation in a good way. People usually get extremely anxious. You need to breathe and believe. Every situation gets better with time and patience.

If you are angry with someone or someone is angry with you, irrespective of what act was done by whom, the dust will settle down someday. You will start recollecting and thinking about the good times. Remember that, one incident doesn't make you a bad person or somebody else, a bad person.

One crisis does not make your life bad. There's always a way to make things better (if you want to make things better). And for that, it is very important to let the dust settle down first. Wait until the time, place and situation seems perfect to give another try or for you to take any decision.

Impulsive people take decisions or react very quickly when something happens. Though some situations truly need a spontaneous reaction, there are many other cases wherein calmness and patience are needed.

I remember few days back I wasn't feeling alright. It was an afternoon. I was feeling upset and anxious because I had a fight with my friend and I was regretting few things. Regret puts you in such a tight situation where you want to punish or curse yourself. But instead of doing that, I listened to meditation music alone in my bedroom. Believe me, it was immensely therapeutic. Those 15 minutes made me so calm and I was back to normal. It also made me think that someday things will get back to normal or at least, I will be able to handle myself or the situation in a better manner. Someday, the dust will settle down and this bitter memory won't bother or hurt both of us. Things change. Situations change. Circumstances change.

Every person wants to think about good memories. No one wants to keep on holding grudges and anger against anyone. Till the time the dust gets settled, it is important for you to make yourself better or your life better.

Why?

Why the focus should be on you?

Don't you think you should keep on apologizing or keep on trying to make things better?

NO. I think we all continuously poke a person and disturb them while we do all these. Therefore, the only thing to do if you want to make things better is to stay calm and not spoil the mental peace of the other person. When we don't allow the situation to settle down and want everything to get better immediately, we don't do the right thing.

That's not a permanent solution to any situation. Good things need good time.

And if we force them to recall only about that incident, things get worse. For them to realise and remember about the positive aspects about your friendship and your bond, you need to give them a lot of space. That is when a person realizes where the loopholes were and things could get better if they see a positive change within you.

Nobody wants to experience the same incident again.

Nobody wants a weak and vulnerable person to build with or share friendship with. We all want a strong and confident friend or partner who can handle every situation maturely.

If you are going through or if you ever happen to go through any bitter experience or uncertainty, remember that few days later, this would fade away and you will feel much better about yourself and your life. Life will keep on giving you shocks. Many things happen which are not according to our expectations and that should be okay and it should be accepted by us.

There are people who lose a lot of money when they invest in stock market. Things fluctuate there. Uncertainties are extremely high. But they handle the situation themselves. Don't they? Initially they feel devastated. But slowly, they realise that uncertainties are part of life. They learn through their mistakes. Things get much clearer when the dust settles down and when you stay calm and composed. And it's not that they stop investing completely. They might take a break, but then they invest smartly and more vigilantly.

You must never restrict yourself.

Give yourself chances when you have clear ideas about the situations. Take decisions or conclude the situations when everything gets settled.

www.ingramcontent.com/pod-product-compliance
Lightning Source LLC
La Vergne TN
LVHW010454160826
845677LV00012B/2476

* 9 7 8 9 3 9 0 5 6 7 5 4 6 *